Book 1
Open Source
By Solis Tech

&

Book 2
Raspberry Pi 2
By Solis Tech

Book 1
Open Source
By Solis Tech

Understanding Open Source From the Beginning!

Open Source: Understanding Open Source From the Beginning!

Table Of Contents

Introduction

I want to thank you and congratulate you for purchasing the book, *"Open Source: Understanding Open Source From the Beginning!"*

This book contains the basics in understanding the open source concept. What is it all about? Where did it come from? Who creates the open source content? How can software be considered as an 'open source'? What makes it different from the other software that we already have?

These questions are answered in this book. Also included in this book are information relevant to open source, such as examples of licensing, the Four Freedoms of free software use, and ideas about software piracy. This information will help to further understand what it means to have some software that is open sourced.

Real life comparisons are also made in this book in case you become confused or lost in understanding the open source concept. The idea of open source seems very simple, but in reality, it is very complex, with definitions coinciding with the definitions of other concepts such as free software (which will further be discussed in Chapter Two). Listed down in the book are the advantages and disadvantages of open source software, and the reasons why more and more people are becoming enticed with the idea of converting to open source.

If the present generation already dictates the movement of open source software, what will become of it in the future? This question is also answered in the last chapter of this book. Due to the fast-paced advancement of technology, open source will adapt to this advancement with the help of both developers and users.

Thanks again for purchasing this book, I hope you enjoy it!

Chapter 1: The Basics of Open Source

Have you ever wondered how an application you're using works? Every time you use an application and it freezes, do you think about what could have gone wrong? Do you ever think of why applications are constantly updating? These are questions that you would not be asked often. But these questions are very important to you, as a user of the Internet age.

Application programs are comprised of source codes, and these source codes are made by programmers. These codes are what allow you to type words into a word processing document, or to click on that video of cats meowing simultaneously. What you see onscreen are only visual representations of the codes of the program. Your application programs may be paid, or pre-installed in your devices, so you don't have permission to view these codes. Rather, you get the pre-made product, and you as a consumer have no power over it except to use it as instructed.

When you purchase or download an application and place it in your device, it installs a lot of files, but none of these files contain the source code. A software manager is included in your installed files to monitor the application as you use it. Whenever your application gets bugged or freezes, this software manager runs, and it prompts you to file a report to the software's developers to tell them exactly what happened. Once the report is filed, the developers study the bug, fix it, and release an update a few days or weeks later.

But what if you could see these codes for yourself? What if, whenever something goes wrong with the application, you could easily contact the developers or ask for help from other programmers easily? These questions are the foundations of open source, and you are about to learn more about it in the following chapters.

What is Open Source?

Open source is a computer program that has its source code visible to the public. The public – which we can refer to as the users – have the power to view, copy, and modify the source codes to their liking. The source code and the compiled version of the code are distributed freely to the users without fixed fees. Users of open source can pretty much do anything they like with the open source programs that they downloaded, since there are practically no restrictions.

To better understand the concept of open source software, let us use an example of recipes for comparison.

Recipes start off with someone writing them down on a piece of paper. A grandma, perhaps, has a recipe for a cake, which she writes in her recipe book. She passes on this recipe to her children, and tells them that they can use the recipe whenever they like. But, they must make sure to credit her as the original creator of the recipe.

The children recreate the recipe and whenever they are asked where the recipe is from, they would always tell that it's from grandma. One of grandma's children alters the cake recipe by adding strawberries as an extra ingredient. The grandma allows this, given that she is also permitted to use the altered recipe.

This example has the same concept with open source software.

When a programmer writes a code, compiles it into a program, and distributes both the source code and the compiled program to the users, he is giving everyone permission to access everything about the program. Users can run the program, view the code, modify if needed, compile, and redistribute the modified version of the program.

The original programmer, however, would require the users to let him use the modified versions of his program, since it is his to begin with. Aside from this certain restriction, the users of the program have the freedom to do whatever they like to do with it.

Let's go back to the example of the cake recipe. One of grandma's children, the one who added the strawberries, suggests to grandma to add the strawberries to the original recipe. The grandma thinks that this is a good idea therefore she complies and replaces her old recipe with the altered cake recipe.

In open source software, if the programmer is notified of a certain modification of a user, and it is deemed to be a modification that the software needs, then the programmer will revise his program based on that certain modification. This modification is called a patch. The user who has suggested of the modification is now coined as a contributor. This process of adapting user modification to an open source software is called upstreaming, because the modification goes back to the original code.

The concept of open source depends on the communication and collaboration between the software's developers and its users. Bug detection and fixing of open source is made easier because numerous users are working simultaneously to study the source code and to compile a modified, fixed version of the code.

With open source, it is not only the developers who are finding new ways on how the software can be improved and upgraded. The users can also contribute their ideas and knowledge in the upgrading of the software. The original developer or programmer can be called the maintainer who monitors the changes in his or her original software.

Let us then go back to the cake recipe. What if another child of grandma decides to do his own version of the cake recipe? He adds raisins to the cake recipe, and asks grandma if the raisins can be added with the strawberries in the original recipe. Grandma refuses, because she dislikes raisins. Instead of being

7

disheartened, this child decides that he would create his own version of the recipe and share it with the people he knows.

If a certain modification makes no appeal to the developer, the one who suggested the modification may opt to make his own version of the program. This act of not patching a modification from the original program is called forking. A forked program is a certain program that alters the original program in such a way that it becomes its own program.

A forked program can be described as a chip off an old block, since it doesn't necessarily separate itself from the license of the program it originated from, although it may seem like it due to the avoidance of patching. Programmers that collaborate with open source result to forking if their modified versions of the original program are deemed unfit by the program's developer.

Nonprofit organizations are the prime developers of open source software. However, due to the freedom of customization that open source has given both users and developers, even large companies are adhering to the open source culture.

How did Open Source become popular?

During the early times of computing, software followed a protocol and design with everyone conforming to a certain cookie-cutter ideal. Software was yet to be imagined as cost-free, and the developers kept their codes to themselves. But then, during the early 90's, the idea of sharing one's code to the public became an accepted idea to most users. The concept of software being free and open sourced became a reality when, after decades, the likes of Mozilla Firefox and OpenOffice were created.

Open source rose in its ranks when developers started making open source alternatives of commercial software. These alternatives are free and can easily be downloaded from the internet, enticing most users to convert to open source. What made open source rise, however, was the idea of community. Fellow programmers could interact and communicate with each other, and even with the developers, which was unheard of during the early times of computing. People could collaborate with the developers of the software and share their insights.

Open source has also given its users the freedom to fully inspect software before they use it – an action that was impossible to do with closed source software. Users who are into coding try open source and study the code line by line.

The popularity of open source software has been anticipated due to the fact that a lot of people supported the cause. Programmers started creating open source projects to contribute to the cause, and users started to get accustomed to obtaining and downloading open source software. With volunteers signing up left and right, and organizations creating their own programs, the growth and expansion of open source software cannot be stopped anymore.

Chapter 2: History, Comparisons, and Relevance

Open source was not immediately implemented until the early 90's, where more and more people began to realize the importance of being able to share the source code of software without fees and royalties. Like any other idea, open source started out as a small thought of making software free for the public, and grew into the culture that it is today.

The History of Open Source: The Open Source Initiative

Eric Raymond, an American software developer, published an essay (turned book) entitled The Cathedral and the Bazaar in 1997. The essay speaks about two different types of software, which he labels the Cathedral and the Bazaar.

In the essay, Raymond describes the Cathedral to be the type of software in which with each release of software, the source code of the software will be available. However, with each build of the software, the certain code block that has been modified is restricted to only the developers of the software. The examples presented under the Cathedral type of software were GNU Emacs (a type of text editor) and the GNU Compiler Collection (a compiler that caters to different programming languages).

In contrast, the Bazaar is the type of software that has the Internet as the venue for their development, making the code visible to the public. The example presented under the Bazaar type of software was Linux (now a widely known computer operating system), in which Raymond coined the developer Linus Torvalds to be the creator of the Bazaar type of software.

Raymond's article became popular in 1998, getting the attention of major companies and fellow programmers. Netscape was influenced by this article, leading them to release the source codes of their internet suite called Netscape Communicator. The source code of the said internet suit was what gave birth to internet browsers such as Thunderbird and SeaMonkey. Mozilla Firefox, a popular web browser today, was also based from the source codes of Netscape Communicator.

The idea of source codes being free became widespread when Linux was developed, urging people to contribute to the open source cause. Because of the increasing popularity of Linux and similar projects, people who became interested in the cause formed the Open Source Initiative, a group whose advocacy is to tell people about the benefits of open sourcing and why it is needed in the computing world.

Open Source vs. Free Software

Most people confused open source software with free software, as the two terms share somewhat the same advocacy. With understanding, it is not that difficult to tell these two terms apart.

The difference between free software and open source software can be listed down into different points. Although they have their differences, both free software and open source software have a singular goal – to publicize source codes for the users to see.

Free software focuses mainly on the ethical aspect of the advocacy. There are certain freedoms that free software are fighting for when it comes to the use of software, which cannot be given to the users by commercial software. These are the Four Freedoms of software use according to advocates of free software:

• The freedom to use the software. This means that the user is free to use the software to his or her needs, or as instructed.

• The freedom to study the source codes of the software. Since the codes are readily available for public viewing, the user has the freedom to view and study the said codes. After he or she reviews the codes, he or she then has the freedom to do the next step.

• The freedom to modify the source codes of the software to the user's liking. If necessary, the user has the freedom to customize the source code and to create a version of the program fit for the user's specific needs.

• The freedom to share the modified, compiled source codes to the public. If the program has been modified, the user has the freedom to compile and publish the modified program for the benefit of the other users who may also have the need of the program's modification. The developer of the original program should also be given the freedom and right to use the modified version of the program.

Free software allows its users to do whatever they want with a program. If they want to modify the source code and redistribute the modified code as their own, without the consent of the original developers, then they are free to do so. If the user wishes to use the source code as the base code of a new project that they are working on, then they will not be sued. The ethical reasoning of free software simply states that there are no grave restrictions when it comes to copying, revising, and republishing the already existing software.

Open source, on the other hand, creates programs with the Four Freedoms in mind. The programs which are considered open source are made for the user's convenience and benefit. The common idea of open source is a group of people working on a single open source project, attempting to create a program that will be beneficial to them, as well as the users.

Open Source and Paid Software

Open source software did indeed come from paid software. There are countless of open source alternatives for common, commercially-sold software readily available on the internet. Some examples of this are office suites like LibreOffice and OpenOffice, which are open source alternatives for the much more popular Microsoft Office.

The reason why open source alternatives of paid software exist is mainly the cost. Users would opt to pay less, or none at all, for certain software. Why pay for software when there are free alternatives that can be downloaded from the internet easily? Open source makes it possible for users who cannot afford paid software to experience the basic and intermediate features of the software, without sacrificing the quality of the end product.

Although open source may be the overall solution for users to get a feel of certain software, there are still others who would want to obtain paid software but through illegal means. This is called software piracy, an action that is still evident despite it being illegal in most countries.

Software piracy is the act of downloading or installing a paid software illegally, either through software cracks or illegally burned CDs. The most popular way to obtain pirated software is through downloading Torrent-based software crack, in which the user can get the files through different computers almost discreetly. Since these software are pirated, installing these software requires the user to turn off his or her Internet connection before installing, to avoid being tracked.

Some paid software can be bought once, and shared with different computers or devices. All of the information regarding the sharing of paid software can be found on the software's End User License Agreement or EULA. The EULA is a splash screen shown at the start of the software's installation which contains the contract between the software's developers and the user.

The EULA may allow the user to share one copy of the software to different devices, or it may restrict the user from doing so. Once the user has violated this part of the EULA, it can then be considered as software piracy.

Something that a user should be aware of is a certain license called the GNU General Public License, the license that most open source software adhere to. The license permits the user to copy, modify, and redistribute the modified code, just as long as the source files and the original codes are still documented. This is important in understanding how and why open source software is allowed to move freely across the internet without being coined as software piracy, as compared to paid, propriety software.

With propriety or paid software, the user is buying only the license. He is not allowed to revise the code, to reverse-engineer the code, and to view the code by

11

all means. The only thing that the user is allowed to do when he purchases propriety software is to use a copy of the software that the developer has provided. It may seem like an unfair deal to some people, because a user should be able to own something that he has paid for.

Open source software changes that idea. It gives the user the freedom to see the program's source code, letting the user know the program's 'skeletal system'. Even without paying for the software, the user gets the full potential functions of the software and not just an executable copy of it.

Importance of Open Source

Technology is rapidly changing. Experts are coming up with more ways to improve the lives of other people. It is the same with those who contribute to open source projects. Their advocacy is to create free programs that will benefit the users.

Open source is important in the evolution of quality software. With a lot of people contributing to one singular project, the software that is produced will be the best of its kind as it has been meticulously observed and reviewed by the contributors. Open source gives way for the collaborative effort of different programmers and users, with the users being secondary developers of a certain program. It is an interactive effort, with the users being able to update the program alongside the developers themselves.

The fast paced advancement of technology would often overwhelm content creators to the point that they would stop creating content altogether. Content creators who are left behind by technology's advancement are often working in small groups or on their own, and have no means of help from fellow creators of their kind.

With Open source, this is never the case. Each open source software has its own community to back a fellow programmer up during each build, ready to help out other programmers and users when needed. The open source community's bond with each other is what makes open source catch up with the fast advancement of technology.

Chapter 3: The Benefits and the Downsides of Open Source

The Benefits of Open Source

The most obvious perk of having open source software is the availability of the source code. With the source code available to the general public, people are able to study the code line by line. Students of programming can study the source code and implement some blocks of it into their own projects, honing their skills and improving their code. Users who are meticulous with their software can view the codes and customize the said codes to their liking.

Aside from the source codes being publicized, another perk of having open source software is that it is mostly free, depending on the software's license. Users of open source software do not have to pay a large sum of money to be able to enjoy the full functions of the software. If the license requires the user to pay, the user may still try out the software's full functions before purchasing.

Open source promotes community. If a user encounters a problem with the downloaded software, he or she can seek help from fellow programmers or the developers themselves through a forum. Users and programmers alike can communicate and share their experiences with using the software, helping other users to get used to the software. With other programmers keen on editing and revising the source code, updated and better versions of the software can easily be uploaded and shared within the community for the benefit of the other users.

Also, when something goes wrong with the open source software, the user has the option to fix the problem himself should seeking help be an option that is not convenient for him. In propriety software, this cannot be possible as the license and copyright prohibits its users from ever touching the program's source code.

If the user of propriety software does as much as reverse-engineer the product, then they could be violating the program's copyright and therefore, be taken to jail. Open source software removes this restriction from the users, giving them permission to fix solvable program problems on their own.

The benefits of open source software are not limited to personal use. Companies and businesses are adhering to the open source paradigm due to the endless possibilities at half the price or lesser.

More and more businesses are converting to open source mainly because it is more cost-efficient than purchasing commercial software. Companies also have more freedom with open source software in terms of customization, since they have the power to mold the software to fit their company's needs. These factors are beneficial in the growth and development of businesses in such a way that the businesses need not to put out a large sum of money just to be able to acquire a software that will be utilized in their business.

Open sourcing has become a way for people to have access to the things that they initially did not have access to. Users of software now have the ability to study the source code of the program they are using, and to know how exactly a certain function of the program runs by looking at its specific line of code.

A sense of community is also created between the software's developers and programmers from outside of their firms. Through open sourcing, the developers are able to communicate with other programmers with regards to how the software can be enhanced further.

Some users would say that using open source operating systems grants more security as compared to paid operating systems. For example, if a user installs the Linux operating system, he or she does not need an antivirus or a virus detection software to keep his or her files intact. The operating system itself has security measures for the user. This becomes a benefit for both professional and nonprofessional users because they have more room for important files rather than installing different kinds of applications for protection.

Open source software is made for the people, by the people. It hones itself to the needs and wants of each user. Because of this, there is no need for the user to upgrade his or her hardware every time the software upgrades.

Take Apple's OSX (operating system) for example. Certain updates of the operating system are available to download, with better features than the previous build. However, older versions of the Macbook and the iMac cannot avail of the recent builds as their hardware are not fit enough to accommodate either the size of the downloaded file or the features itself.

With open source software, the upgrades can be coded to fit each user's needs, depending on the user's hardware. If a certain upstreamed version of the open source software is available to download, different downloaders are made available by the developer with the specifications listed beside each downloader, catering to the different specifications of the user. The user himself can opt to customize the code of the program to be compatible with his device.

Allowing the user these freedoms over the software has given open source software a bit of a leverage over paid, propriety software. But then again, there will be nay-sayers who think that open source software isn't the way to go.

The Downsides and Disadvantages of Open Source

Open sourcing has given users lots of benefits, but it is not perfect. Some would still prefer paid software over any open sourced software. Here are some of the reasons why some users do not approve of open source.

If a user is not in any way a technology expert, he or she would want software that is easy to use. Open source software is known to be more technical compared to their paid counterparts. Paid software focuses on its user interface, making the application easy for the user to understand the system. Open source software usually start out with a not so attractive user interface, but with the basic functions of the program intact. As the program gets updated with each build, the user interface changes and adapts to the needs of its users.

Most critics would say that paid or propriety software is still better in a number of factors as compared to open source software. Because more people are accustomed to using paid or propriety software, the idea that there are other types of software available is intimidating to them. People think that open source software is made only for the technology savvy users, with the interface hard for them to manipulate. Why download a complicated software when they can buy a simple, pre-made software that they are already familiar with?

Paid software has become a norm in the everyday lives of users. Large companies such as Microsoft and Apple have made their name known all throughout the world, creating technologies that users and consumers have grown to love. Because of their undying popularity, the rise of open source software is unknown to the general public. And even if they are known, those who are used to seeing the big names are hesitant to try out what open source might be.

Seeking technical help might seem simple with the numerous open source communities readily available, but it may sometimes be inconvenient to the user. Paid software offer professional tech support straight from the manufacturers.

Chapter 4: The Open Source Culture

Open source gives the user freedom to do whatever he or she wants in a software. Who wouldn't want the freedom to edit source codes to their own liking? With open source, this opportunity of customization is available at hand.

Why are more people converting to open source?

With the source code open for public scrutiny, looking for errors will be easier. Other software companies that do not have their source code publicized have their own set of programmers and developers figuring out the bugs in the software. This is an advantage for companies who always require their software to be updated regularly to keep up with the business.

Students who cannot afford the luxury of paid software turn to their open source counterparts to be able to utilize their functions without having to pay a large amount of money. Open source alternatives of Microsoft Office are available for the students to download should they need to use an office suite for their projects.

Some open source versions of paid software are actually better. Paid media players can play certain file types and extensions, but crash once the file extension is unrecognizable. Open source software developers take note of these bugs and create a media player that can play almost all media file types and extensions in high definition. Because of this, even users who are not actually technology savvy would convert to the open source alternatives of paid software just because they've heard and they know that they can get more out of the open source counterpart.

Programmers who want to practice their coding also rely on readily available open source software in their study. Because the codes of open source can easily be viewed and modified, programmers can base their project on open source software and publish it as their own, creating a program fork.

Businesses, on the other hand, turn to open source software for two main factors: cost efficiency and the power of customization. As mentioned in a previous chapter, with open source software readily available to download on the internet, the businesses do not need to spend a lot of money for a software that they cannot customize as their own. Open source gives them the opportunity to keep on upgrading their system as needed, therefore improving the quality of their software with each build.

The flexibility of open source software has enticed businesses to change to open source from propriety software. Businesses would often buy already existing software and attempt to use them as instructed by the developers. Open source software has its own rules and regulations, but if businesses want their software to be something specific, then the developers of open source software will deliver. With propriety software, the business is the one to adjust to the software that they have purchased, an action that is removed once businesses convert to open source.

Examples of Open Source Software

A wide variety of open source software are available for download. These software may be used for utility purposes, for multimedia purposes – anything that the user desires and requires. Here are a few examples of open source software that you as a user have probably heard of.

The prime example of open source software is an operating system called Linux. It is an operating system based off of UNIX that is available to different computer platforms and hardware.

Another example of open source software is the media player called VLC Media Player developed by the VideoLAN Organization. This media player can run a variety of multimedia files at high definition. Its paid counterpart is Microsoft's own Windows Media Player, which before its most recent build can only play a handful of file extensions.

When it comes to operating systems, Android is another popular example of open source software. A company called Android, Inc. (later bought by Google) has developed this mobile operating system using another open source kernel, Linux. It caters mostly to devices which have touchscreen on them, such as touchscreen desktop monitors, tablets, and smartphones, much like its counterpart from Apple called iOS. Android has its own application store called Google Play, where the users can install applications onto their phones mostly for free.

Netbeans, a well-known software developing application, is also an example of an open source software. It is a Java-created application that caters to different programming languages, and can be run on multiple operating systems. Programmers use Netbeans to create object oriented applications using the 24 programming languages that it caters to.

GIMP, or GNU Image Manipulation Program, is an Adobe Photoshop-like application that edits photos and creates graphic images. It has basic photo editing features such as cropping, grayscaling, and resizing, making it a simpler alternative to Photoshop. Like its paid counterpart, users of GIMP can also create animated GIF images, a feature that most multimedia artists are very fond of using.

Video and computer games can also be open sourced. Some open source games such as Tux Racer are available in the Linux package when downloaded. The principle of open source games is the same as any other open source software – the developers merging and collaborating with the users to create quality content to be distributed to the general public. However, the visual quality and elements of open source games are yet to be improved.

Other examples include PHP (a web development language), MySQL (used in databases alongside applications such as Microsoft Access and Microsoft Visual Basic), Python (programming language), Blender (an Autocad Maya-esque application that caters to 3D rendering), and many more.

Chapter 5: The Future of Open Source

What will happen in the future?

The future of open sourcing seems bright. With most businesses converting to open source software and most developers contributing to open source projects, the growth and expansion of open sourcing will continue. Open sourcing gives way for the innovation of modern software technology – with a lot of people working on one simple open source project, there is no doubt that the project will continue to be updated and improved.

Software will only continue to improve as time passes by. Open source software has made it easier for software to improve and upgrade itself due to countless of volunteers who are up to the challenge. While propriety software claim to start software trends, open source software advocates the upgrades of software that will be favorable to the needs of the users rather than to the bank accounts of the developers.

Open source software does not wish to waste the time and money of the user; rather, it aims to maximize both time and money, with the inclusion of effort, of the user when utilizing the software.

Presently, paid software are still dominant over open source software. Paid software have more leverage compared to open source software when it comes to reliability and familiarity, since they have been used by programmers and users alike for decades. There is still a certain percentage of users who are not aware that there are open source versions of their paid software, which they can help improve and customize to their own needs and liking.

More people will be aware of the benefits of open source software in the future. With propriety software releasing more licenses that restrict its users from certain software freedom, the existence of open source will lead to the users converting from propriety software due to the lack of free will.

In the future, there is a possibility that open source will be available not just for software, but also for other forms of content that have sources.

The future of open source as an idea or a paradigm will not be restricted to software alone. With the further advancement of technology, more and more gadgets will be locked down by licenses and warranties which restrict its users from fixing even simple problems that the product may have.

Gadgets are becoming more and more digitized, and copyright restricts people from ever touching or attempting to change the software. Because of this, some people are beginning to open up to the idea of open source not just for software, but also for hardware and gadgets that are used every day.

Open Source: Understanding Open Source From the Beginning!

Let us take tractors for example. Tractors are machines that are essential in farming. If a tractor breaks down, the farmer himself can fix the broken tractor and keep it running again without having to buy a new one. But the modernization of technology leads the manufacturers of tractors to add digital aspects into their products: tractors now have microchips and are operated via computers, therefore are now protected by copyright.

Now, if the new tractor breaks down, the farmer has no permission to fix the tractor himself. He must hire a specialist to fix the problem, or else he goes to jail.

Open source hardware has already started to rise in its ranks alongside open source software. It basically means that users are free to create their gadgets from scratch, using open source hardware. Although the idea seems taboo at present, the fact that gadgets are also being restricted from the users will give way for both open source hardware and software to rise even further, giving users complete freedom over the creation and implementation of the technology that they need.

Content creators are restricted from creating certain things just because of copyright laws. Even artists, who upload videos on websites like YouTube and Vimeo, get flagged just because of a certain song or a certain speech that had some sort of copyright over it. This restricts creative freedom. It also restricts the content creators from creating what they know and love, and sharing it with their viewers.

Will open sourcing become a culture in the future? Surely, with the massive amounts of information available for the users to share freely amongst themselves. Open source software has given way for an idea that will change the world of computing for everyone, and allows everyone to have access to the large chunk of information that was previously not available to them. Transparency when it comes to creating code and building machines will become a fad in the future, as more and more people are willing and able to create content and share it with other users.

Conclusion

Thank you again for purchasing this book!

I hope this book was able to help you to understand better the concept of open source and its benefits to the public.

Finally, if you enjoyed this book, please take the time to share your thoughts and post a review on Amazon. It'd be greatly appreciated!

Thank you and good luck!

Book 2

Raspberry Pi 2

By Solis Tech

Raspberry Pi 2 Programming Made Easy!

Raspberry Pi 2: Raspberry Pi 2 Programming Made Easy!

Table of Contents

Introduction

Greetings. Thank you for purchasing this book Raspberry Pi 2: Raspberry Pi 2 Programming Made Easy. If you're reading this book then most likely you are here to learn about his nifty new little computer called the Raspberry Pi. In this book, we'll teach you everything that you need to know to get up and running with this little, but powerful computer.

We'll teach you about its parts, its specifications, setting up the operating system, its capabilities and limitations, and ultimately how to do basic programming. We'll discuss the best programming language that works best with the Raspberry Pi and create your first program with it. Without further ado, let's start your Raspberry Pi journey.

Chapter 1: Raspberry Pi – The Basics

What is a Raspberry Pi?

So what is it exactly? We'll it's a small credit-card sized single board computer that is intended to help people learn more about programming, how the computer works, etc. The CPU or Central Processing Unit is basically a system-on-a-chip. What that means is it pairs an ARM processor that is used by a lot of embedded systems and cellular phones with a Broadcom GPU (Graphics Processing Unit), which is a fairly powerful graphics processor that's capable of displaying full resolution 1080p HD video.

The amount of RAM (Random Access Memory) that the Raspberry Pi 2 has is 1 Gigabyte. Its previous iteration, the Raspberry Pi 1 Model A+ and Raspberry Pi 1 Model B has 256MB and 512MB RAM respectively. The RAM is shared by both the CPU and the GPU.

The Raspberry Pi 2 starts at $39.00 and that includes just the board. On the board there are 4 USB ports, 40 General Purpose Input/Output (GPIO) pins, a full 1080p HDMI port, a Network/Ethernet port, a 3.5mm audio and composite video jack, a Raspberry Pi (CSI) Camera interface, a Video (DSI) Display interface, a Micro SD card slot, and a VideoCore 3D graphics core. The GPIO is basically for more advanced users who are going to be adding Arduino accessory boards, ribbon cables for communication with other hardware devices, and major electronics projects; robotics, sensors, etc.

Why Is it Cool to Have a Raspberry Pi?

Most people think the Raspberry Pi is cool because it's a fairly complete computer, it runs on very little power, it's small, and it will not burn a hole through your wallet; it's $39.00, which is less than the cost that you would pay for a dinner with a friend or a loved one. The Raspberry Pi also helps people that are new to computer hardware get into it and get their hands dirty without the cost and risk associated with more expensive standard hardware.

Another thing that's cool about it is that the Graphics Processing Unit is pretty powerful. It can play 1080p HD video, which makes it really attractive to a lot of people as a Media Center PC. In fact, most people buy the Raspberry Pi 2 for that specific reason because it is a cheap multimedia PC.

What Can You Do With a Raspberry Pi?

So what can you do with this thing? Well, just like what was previously mentioned, if you're really new to computer hardware, the Pi can help you learn about those individual components of most modern computers. And if you want to learn how to do programming, the Raspbian operating system that comes with the Raspberry Pi 2 comes with a lot of tools for programming to help you get started.

So you might be asking, why wouldn't you start learning how to program with the computer that you already have? Well, you can. And that's perfectly fine. However, you can think of the Raspberry Pi as your little playground and your test computer that you don't have to worry about breaking if you screw something up. Even if you do break it, you'll only be losing $39.00.

But if you don't care about all that and you don't care about programming or about learning the hardware and so forth, the Raspberry Pi 2 also makes a really great little Media PC. You can get a small case for it, hook it up to the network, install another operating system that's based on Linux called OpenELEC, which is basically a back-end for XBMC (Xbox Media Center), plug it into your TV, and you're ready to start streaming video and audio content on your high-definition TV.

Chapter 2: Hardware Accessories

In this chapter, we're going to talk about some of the hardware and accessories that you're going to need to get started with the Raspberry Pi 2. First, let's start out with the bare necessities. The two things that you'll definitely need are power and an SD card.

Power Requirement

Let's take a moment here and talk about power because it's important. The Raspberry Pi is a little picky about its power source. Learning about what you need here for power could save you a lot of headache later down the road. The Raspberry Pi needs 5 volts. That should be anywhere between 4.75 volts minimum and a maximum of 5.25 volts. It should be at least 700 mAh, but the recommended is 1000 mAh.

The reason for the 1000 mAh recommended power is because when you start plugging in a keyboard, mouse, network cable, and other peripherals, these all pull power away from the system. This is also why some Raspberry Pi 2 users say that 1500 mAh to 2000 mAh is even better. Of course, if you're only doing projects close to your desktop computer and you don't really plan to run the Raspberry Pi 24/7, you could just run it off of your desktop system's power with just a USB cable if you want.

SD Card Storage

There is not on-board storage on the Raspberry Pi. So you need an SD card to run the operating system from and also to store any files. Get at least the Class 4 SD storage. It is recommended that you get the Class 6 or Class 10 if you don't mind spending a little bit more.

However, if it's not available, just get the best one that you can. The cost difference honestly isn't that much, and SD cards are getting cheaper all the time. You'll also need a card reader to transfer the operating system image that you're going to download off of Raspberry Pi's website from your desktop computer to the SD card. You can also buy SD cards with the operating system pre-installed from whosoever your Raspberry Pi vendor is if ever you want to skip the operating system installation on the Pi.

If you want to try out multiple operating systems, you can do that with a single card. However, just keep in mind that you'll overwrite any of your settings that you've played around with in the operating system.

Interacting With the Raspberry Pi

You'll need to decide on how you want to interact with your Raspberry Pi. You can either do it headless over a network, with a keyboard, mouse and monitor, or you can do a combination of both. For network access, you're going to need a network cable; either a CAT5e or CAT6 to connect to your router. There's also a USB WiFi option, which allows you to connect to your router wirelessly.

If you're going headless, you don't really need a USB keyboard and mouse. They are both optional. It just depends on what you want to use the Raspberry Pi for. Just like what was previously mentioned, if you don't want to use the desktop interface, you can skip using a mouse and just plug in a keyboard. If you're using it as a media center and navigate XBMC, a wireless Bluetooth keyboard is a fantastic option if you want to sit on your couch and navigate your media center.

If you're only planning to login remotely using SSH, you can skip the keyboard entirely, or if you want you can just borrow a keyboard and mouse from another machine for the initial setup before you actually go headless over the network. Raspberry Pi should automatically get an IP address from your router. After your router gives an IP address to your Pi, you can just log in to your router to see the exact IP address that was assigned. You can then connect via SSH using that IP address.

If you don't want to find out what the exact IP address is via the router and instead want to find it out locally, you can pull up the command terminal in Raspbian OS and execute an "ifconfig" command. You can then unplugged your peripherals and go headless from there.

Displays

Moving on to displays, if your TV or monitor has an HDMI input, that's great because all you'll need to get is a cheap HDMI cable. If your monitor only has DVI-in, you'll need an HDMI to DVI cable or an adapter. Just keep in mind that if you do that, the audio signal that's coming out of the HDMI port will be ignored when you're using a DVI converter.

Depending on your setup, you can use external speakers or a splitter. If you're going to go headless, you can skip purchasing a separate monitor specifically for your Pi and just borrow one for the initial setup if you want to. Otherwise, you can still do most of the setup across the network if you are connected via SSH.

Raspberry Pi Casing

Moving forward, even though it may look cool keeping your bare board out with a bunch of wires just hanging off, it is probably not the safest thing to do for your Raspberry Pi. So it is recommended that you get a case for your Pi. You can get a prefab case for as little as $5.00. It is completely optional but it does help protect the board. A number of people have made some pretty cool custom cases, all of which are available for purchase on-line.

Chapter 3: Installing the Operating System In Your SD Card

In this chapter we're going to be looking at operating system options and how to actually install it in your Raspberry Pi. First off, you're going to need to consider what your goal is for your Raspberry Pi. Is this going to be a learning or tinkering board? Are you going to be programming or do you just want a quick and cheap home theater PC? For a more general purpose operating system or for the tinkerer and programmer, most people recommend going for Raspbian OS.

The latest version of Raspbian at the time of this writing is Raspbian Jessie Kernel Version 4.1, which was released in November 2015. For a home theater PC, most people recommend getting either OpenELEC or RaspBMC. If you're just not sure and you want to try multiple operating system versions, get two or three SD cards and you can just install a different operating system on each of them. You can swap them out depending on what you feel like doing with your Raspberry Pi. Below is the link where you can download the various operating systems for your Pi:

https://www.raspberrypi.org/downloads/

The Operating system installation method that we're about to discuss is mainly for those who have a Mac or a Linux desktop. If you have Windows, the concept is still pretty much the same. You'll just use a different program to get the disk image onto your SD card with Windows.

Step 1

Regardless of which type of PC you're using, you're going to need to download the disk image or images of your preferred operating system for your Raspberry Pi. These are by no means the only options, just the ones that the Raspberry Pi community recommends in order to get you started. The first one, as we've mentioned before, is Raspbian.

There's also another version that came out called Occidentalis, which is actually based on Raspbian but has a more educational slant to it and includes a lot more educational tools. For a home theater PC, you'll want to install either OpenELEC or RaspBMC. Both of these are built around the XBMC (Xbox Media Center).

Step 2

Once you have chosen your operating system, click the download link and choose a location in your computer that you're going to easily remember. Once your download is complete, it would probably be in a .zip file format so you'll need to unzip it and you should now have an image file with an .img file extension. There are a lot of different methods to get this image onto the SD card, but if you're on Linux or Mac, we're just going to use the "dd" command to write the image on the card.

We're going with this method mainly because it's installed in almost every UNIX-based system and it should work pretty much the same on all of them. Before we proceed in talking about DD in Mac or Linux, if you're a Windows PC user, you're going to need to download the win32 disc imager. Once you've installed it, you need to run it and tell it where the operating system image file is located on your hard drive and what drive letter to write the image to for your SD card.

When choosing the actual drive letter that points to your SD card, make sure that the SD card you're using is blank since everything inside it is going to be overwritten. Getting back to Linux and Mac, you want to open up a new shell or a terminal as it's called on the Mac, and then navigate to the folder where you downloaded your disk image. In most cases it would be in /Downloads/Raspberry Pi/Raspbian.

Again, keep in mind that you will be overwriting everything on the SD card that you're going to be using for this installation. So use a fresh card or one you don't mind overwriting. At this point, make sure you do not have your SD card reader plugged in yet. The reason for this is because we need to find out which device our SD card will be using.

In your terminal or shell, type "df" (without the quotes) and then press ENTER. Now you should see a list of devices and the folders where they are mounted. This should be any of your internal hard drives or external hard drives and so forth. Now is the time when you want to plug in your SD card into your reader and then plug the reader into an open USB port.

Just wait a few moments for the card to mount. This can take a few seconds. After a few seconds, use the "df" command again. You should now see something different; an item that's listed as either no-name or volume/untitled. On the side you should see something listed like dev/disk3s1 or on Linux it would be something similar to dev/sdb1 or sdc1 or something like that next to it.

Drive assignments may vary from user to user so just take which device is listed next to that volume carefully. You want to make sure that you're using the SD device and not one of your hard drives. DD is an unforgiving command and it will overwrite without prejudice and without asking you if you're sure about doing so. So just be very careful. We can't stress this enough. You don't want to overwrite your main hard drive.

Once you know the device that you're going to write to, remember or write it down. Like what we mentioned earlier, it should be something like dev/disk3s1 on a Mac or something similar to dev/sdc1 on Linux. We're going to change this a little bit since we actually want to write the disk image to the entire card not just a partition on the card, which is what we have mounted right now.

So what we need to do now is unmount the SD card's partition before we can write to the entire card. We don't want to eject the card, we just want to unmount it. On your Mac you can open up your Disk Utility. It's in the same folder as your terminal. You then have to select the volume under the SD card device and click "unmount." You can also do this from the terminal, but you'll need to be on the superuser account. So to use Disk Utility using a superuser or root account, you can type the command below:

$ sudo diskutil unmount/dev/disk3s1

On Linux you would do a similar thing. You would type in the command below:

$ sudo unmount /dev/sdc1

You can type the command above or whatever your device assignment happens to be. One thing to remember is that the sudo command will always ask you for the administrator password in order to be able to execute the command, regardless of whether you're using a Mac or a Linux system. Once the SD card's partition is unmounted, we're going to run DD with 3 arguments; "bs," "if," and "of." Those stand for block size, in file, and out file respectively. You'll run the command exactly as below:

$ dd bs=1m if=2015-12-24-jessy-raspbian.img of=/dev/sdc1

Looking at the command above, you're going to be putting a value for block size; specifically 1m which stands for 1 megabyte, for "if" you'll be putting the name of the image file, and "of" is the location where you stored the image file. Regarding the location of the image file, we're going to change that a little bit. For example, if your device is listed as /dev/disc3s1, you want to change the "of" argument to /dev/rdisk3s1.

This may be different depending on your system so changing this will make sure that you use the entire SD card and not just the partition. In Linux for example, the "of" value would probably be something like /dev/sdb1 or /dev/sdc1. In this case, the letter after the letters "sd" could be different depending on your system. So in order to write to the whole card, you just need to take away the number "1." You should have something similar to the one below:

$ dd bs=1m if=2015-12-24-jessy-raspbian.img of=/dev/sdb

So that's pretty much of it. Once you're confident that you have the correct arguments for the DD command, hit ENTER. You're going to wait a few minutes while the SD card is being written on. At this point, you won't see any output while this process is ongoing. It will probably take a few minutes so just be patient.

If you're on Linux and you get an error, you might need to change the "bs" value from 1m to 1M (capital M). For some reason the case of the letter matters to a Linux system. Once this has been completed, you should be back to a command prompt. And assuming everything worked properly, you will now have a bootable operating system on your SD card.

You are now ready to boot your Raspberry Pi for the first time and start configuring your system, which we will cover on the next chapter.

Chapter 4: Booting OpenELEC & Raspbian for the First Time On Your Pi

In the last chapter, we installed the operating system on the SD card. Let's now go ahead and insert the SD card into the slot on the underside of the Raspberry Pi. Keep in mind that the metal contacts of the SD card should be facing the underside of the board. First, we'll need at least a keyboard, a mouse, and a monitor. Go ahead and plug the keyboard and mouse to any of the available USB ports. Second, go ahead and plug in the Ethernet CAT5 or CAT6 cable on the Ethernet port on the Pi. Make sure that the other end of the Ethernet cable is plugged into your router. Third, go ahead and plug in the HDMI cable for your monitor.

Do not forget to use an HDMI to DVI converter if you have a DVI monitor. Lastly, plug in the microUSB cable of the 5V power supply to the microUSB port on your Raspberry Pi. Once you have everything plugged in, you should see the LEDs on the board start to light up. You will also see that the boot cycle has now started on the monitor. Just wait for login prompt to appear once the boot process has finished.

Logging In

Once you have the login prompt, you want to use the default username which is "pi", and the default password, which is "raspberry" in all lower case. Once you type those in and press ENTER, you're in.

To start the desktop interface just type "start x" and press ENTER. Most people should be pretty familiar with how this desktop works. It's very similar to most other modern GUI interfaces. Let's now take a look at some of the applications that are available to you once you've successfully started the desktop interface of your Raspberry Pi.

- Scratch – This is basically a programming teaching tool. It is very similar to Karel. If you've ever taken a programming class, they use Karel the robot to teach you basic programming concepts.

- Python – Python is basically a very versatile and robust programming language. It is used by many programmers and companies to make web based applications.

- Midori – Midori is a lightweight web browser. It takes its roots from Mozilla Firefox.

- File Manager – The file manager is very similar to the Window file manager. It lets you see the different directories and storage media that's associated with your Raspberry Pi. It also lets you see the important files in your Raspberry Pi.

- Terminal – Since Raspbian is basically a derivative of Debian Linux, it's no surprise that it also has a terminal similar to Linux. It has the same functions as a Linux terminal. It can also run all the terminal commands that you can run in a Linux system.

Now that we've pretty much seen what the Raspbian operating system looks like, let's go on ahead and see what OpenELEC looks like in a Raspberry Pi. Go ahead and mount the image of OpenELEC onto your SD card. The mounting process for OpenELEC is pretty much the same as Raspbian. If you're still logged into Raspbian on your Raspberry Pi, you must log out and shut the Pi down.

You shut the Raspberry Pi down by using the "halt" command. Again, in order for this command to work, you have to be a superuser. So you need to type in the word "sudo," then put a space by pressing the spacebar, type in the word "halt," and then press ENTER.

After you press ENTER, the Raspberry Pi will initiate the shutdown process. Once finished, you can now switch to the SD card with the OpenELEC operating system. Once the card is inserted, you can start booting your Raspberry Pi with the OpenELEC operating system. As you can see, you can pretty quickly change out cards and be up and running with a different operating system pretty quickly.

Once you have OpenELEC up and running, go ahead and explore the different parts of the operating system, see the different programs it has, and find out what it can do. This is the perfect time to explore and learn what the Raspberry Pi and its operating system is all about.

Chapter 5: How to Get Around in the Raspberry Pi's Unix-based Command Line Interface

In this chapter, we will be going through some of the more basic commands that you're going to need to know in the command line shell for getting around the Unix-based file system. If you're running Raspbian, you'll need to know some of the standard Unix commands. Like most systems in Linux or Unix, files are stored in directory hierarchies.

You can also call them folders if you want to feel more comfortable with that term. When you login, unless you have a custom setting, you will most likely begin in your home/username directory. For Raspbian, the default username that we've been logging in with is Pi. So your home directory is going to be /home/Pi.

Most users on the system, except for root, will have their home directory stored within /home. The main exception is the root user's folder, which is stored in /root. On your command prompt you will see your home directory represented as a tilde symbol "~", and you can use that to easily get back to your home folder anytime.

Moving forward, let's get into working with directories. The first thing you might want to know is where you are and what directory you are located in. The first command that we're going to start with is PWD. PWD stands for Print Working Directory, which tells you the current directory that you're located in at that moment. You'll find that most commands in Unix are abbreviations of the activity that they perform.

As you can see from the output after you typed in PWD and pressed ENTER, you're in /home/pi. If you want to change to another directory, you need to use the CD command. For example, if you want to go to the top level directory—also called the root, which is not to be confused with the root user home directory— you type in this command:

```
$ cd /
```

cd / represents the main directory; and the slash that is used is a forward slash. Many people mistakenly use the term backslash when they really mean forward slash. We call the "/" a forward slash because we read from left to right. So a slash leaning to the right is in the forward direction.

Typing the aforementioned command and pressing ENTER will bring you to the top level directory. There is nothing above this top level directory. It only has subdirectories beneath it. With that being said, let's now take a moment to look at a few subdirectories beneath the main root directory.

The first one that we're going to look at is "etc." Etc stores many of the system's configuration files so get familiar with this folder. If you want to change configuration settings, you're going to come here often. To go to the etc subdirectory from the root directory, type in the command below:

```
$ cd /etc
```

Now let's take a look at what's inside etc. We do that using the "ls" command. Ls is short for list and it just lists directory contents. ls also have some options associated with it that allows the user to change the way the listing looks.

Let's go ahead and take a look at a few common options of ls:

- -a – lists all files including hidden files in the directory. Files beginning with a dot "." are considered hidden. So anything that you name with a dot preceding the file name will be hidden automatically, unless you use the -a option to list the files.

- -l – lists all the files lengthwise down the screen.

- -p – puts a forward slash after the directory, which is inside the current directory that you are viewing. This lets you easily distinguish directories from files.

- --color – this will give you a colorful directory listing. However, this

39

doesn't always work. This command works depending on the system and if you're logging in remotely.

You can also combine multiple options with a single dash. Look at the example below:

$ ls -lap

Typing the command above will give you all the options that you've indicated together with the list command. Now, to go back a directory, you have two options. In this particular case we can either type cd / to take us back to the main root directory since that's where we started before going into etc, or we can type the command below:

$ cd ..

That's "cd" followed by a space, and then two dots. This takes us back one directory. We also have another command below:

$ cd ../..

This command takes us back two directories if you happen to be two subdirectories in. So if you're still in the "etc" directory, go back one directory. There are a number of other directories to familiarize with within the root directory. Below are some of those directories:

- /bin – this directory is for commands and binaries.

- /sbin – this is for system and administrator commands.

- /user – this is for user-related files. It also has its own /bin and /sbin subdirectories.

- /var – var stands for variable. The /var/log subdirectory is a common destination for users who troubleshoot problems whose log file end up here.

- /home – As what we discussed before, this is for the user directories.

- /mnt – mnt, which stands for Mount, is pretty much the mount point for any external drives, image files, or things like that.

- /dev – this is for devices that interface with the hardware.

- /lib – this is for programs and program libraries.

There a lot more, but this is just a quick rundown of the more common directories that you're likely to encounter and use.

So how do we add, remove, or modify files and directories? Well, to create a new directory, type in the command below:

```
$ mkdir directoryname
```

Mkdir stands for make directory. This should be followed by a space and then the name of the directory that you want to create. To remove that empty directory, just used the command below:

```
$ rmdir directoryname
```

Rmdir stands for remove directory. This should be also followed by a space and then the name of the directory that you want to remove. Keep in mind that using this command with a non-empty directory would result to an error. There's another option to remove a directory even though it contains files and subdirectories. However, it can be a little dangerous in the wrong hands if they don't know what they're doing.

So please use with caution whenever you utilize the below command:

$ rm -rf directoryname

The -r option after the remove command means to do the removing process recursively, which drills down into the subdirectories located within the directory you're trying to remove. The -f option stands for Force, which forces the process to go through. So executing this command basically tells the system that you know what you're doing.

The system will allow you to execute the command as long as you have permission to that file or directory. Again, use these options only if you really need to. There won't be any dialogue box, pop-up window, or anything like that to save you from making a mistake with this command.

For copying files and directories, you'll be using the CP command. Look at the example command below:

$ cp filename1 filename2

First type in the cp command, followed by a space, followed by the name of the file to copy from, followed by another space, and then lastly the name of the file to copy to. Note that filename 1 and filename 2 should be different. Also, keep in mind that you need to have root (sudo) access in order to successfully execute this file.

To rename or move a file without duplicating it, use the command below:

$ mv filename1 filename2

The above command will essentially move the contents of filename1 to filename2. You can also specify directories where files are located. For example, let's say you want to copy the contents of /etc/hosts to your home folder. For that you would use the below command:

$ cp /etc/hosts /home/pi

Type in the cp command, followed by a space, then followed by the file-path of the file that you want to copy, and then another space, and then followed lastly by the file-path of the location where you want to copy the file to.

To move or copy a directory and its subdirectories, you want to use the -r option, which is again a recursive option.

$ cp -r directory1 directory2

If you want to find out about any of these commands, you can use the MAN command. MAN stands for manual. If you want to find out more about the cp command for example, you just have to type the command below:

$ man cp

This will pull up all the information about the cp command and all the options associated with it. The same applies to the mv, rm, and so forth.

Chapter 6: Python Programming in Raspberry Pi

In this chapter, we're going to look at the best programming language for the Raspberry Pi; Python. It is considered by many as a notably powerful and dynamic language that is used to develop numerous application domains. Most programmers compare Python to Perl, Java, Ruby, Tcl, or Scheme. This is why Python is the primary language the Raspberry Pi is designed to operate on.

Below are some of the key features of the Python programming language:

- Superb for programming veterans and also remain simple enough for beginners to understand.

- Excellent scalability. Python is excellent in small projects; even better for large scale ones.

- Extremely portable and is compatible across all platforms

- Hardware embeddable

- Elegant and simple to understand syntax and semantics

- Excellent stability

- Has a huge standard library of pre-built subroutines, codes, etc.

Moving forward, we'll discuss how to get a very simple python program working. In addition, we'll also discuss how to use the Graphical User Interface to code basic python programs. However, what this chapter won't tackle is the nitty-gritty of learning how to program in Python. Python object-oriented programming is a whole topic in itself and is therefore out of the scope of this book.

Python programming in the Raspberry Pi is similar to Python programming using a normal desktop or laptop computer. It's just that with the Raspberry Pi, you're programming in a very portable, cheap, but robust platform. To start programming with Python on your Raspberry Pi, you must first make sure that you've successfully installed the Raspbian operating system.

Using the desktop of your Raspbian OS, click on the Menu option on the taskbar. Clicking on menu allows you to see the sub-menus for Raspbian. Click on the "Programming" sub-menu. Once you do that, you'll be presented with different programming applications for Raspbian. One of those applications would be your Python Editor.

Python Editors vary depending on the version of Raspbian running in your Raspberry Pi. However, the most common Python IDE would be Stan's Python Editor or SPE. Click on that and you'll be presented with GUI (Graphical User Interface) for your Python IDE (Integrated Development Environment).

The main window of your Python IDE is where you'll type the source code of the program that you're developing. To start making our simple Python program, first create a folder on your Raspbian desktop where we will put our python script. Just right click on any empty space on your desktop and click "Create New Folder." Don't forget to give your new folder a name.

Now, let's go ahead and develop a simple "Hello World" program using Python. To do so, go to the code editor window of your Python IDE and type in the following code:

```
1       print "Hello World"
```

After typing this code in your editor, save it by clicking on the "File" menu at the menu of your Python IDE and then click on "Save." You will have to give your python script a name. In this case, just type in the filename as HelloWorld.py and save it inside the new folder that you have created on your desktop. Take note that filenames should not contain any spaces and that it should have a .py extension. This is the file extension for all Python scripts.

After saving the file, run the program by clicking on the "run" button on the menu bar of your Python IDE. At this point, two things should happen depending on which Python IDE you're using. Some IDEs will pull up the terminal and display the output of the program from there, while other IDEs will have a status bar at the bottom where it will show you the output of the Python program that you just ran.

Regardless of whatever mode of output your IDE uses, it should display the words "Hello World." If you want to run your Python script from the terminal itself and not from the IDE, all you need to do is navigate to where your Python script is located first and run the script from there. To do this, type the command below:

```
$ cd /home/pi/Desktop/foldername
```

The "foldername" is the name of the folder that you have created on the desktop. Once you're there type the below command to display the contents of that folder:

```
$ ls -l
```

Now, you'll see your HelloWorld.py file. To run this just type in the below command:

```
$ python HelloWorld.py
```

The command above is basically telling the system to use the Python interpreter to open the HelloWorld.py file. Press ENTER and you'll see the output; "Hello World."

Congratulations, you've just made your first Python program in your Raspberry Pi.

Conclusion

Thank you for purchasing and reading this book. We hope that we've taught you all the basic things that you need to know about your Raspberry Pi; how to set it up, how to install the operating system so that you'll be able to develop programs using it.

From here, developing more intricate programs using Python is just a matter of learning the nitty-gritty of the programming language itself. There are many online tutorials out there that you can go and see to get in-depth knowledge of Python programming. Python is a very versatile and stable programming language and using it to make your Pi do wondrous things is easy, as long as you have an advanced knowledge of the programming language itself.

Again, Thank you so much and we hope that you succeed in your quest for knowledge on the Python programming language and that you have fun in finding ingenious ways to use your Raspberry Pi.